Cats: 80 Fascinating Facts For Kids

Anne Walker

This book is just one of a series of "Fascinating Facts For Kids" books. For more fascinating facts about people, history, animals, and more please visit:

www.fascinatingfactsforkids.com

Contents

Introduction

Cats have had a close and affectionate relationship with humans for around 10,000 years, firstly as hunters and later being accepted into homes as pets.

Over the centuries, cats have been worshipped as gods in ancient Egypt and burned alive by Christians in medieval Europe, before becoming the most popular pet in the world today.

We hope the following facts will fascinate you and encourage you to find out more about these remarkable animals.

Anne Walker
October 2014

History & Evolution

1. The first cat-like animals prowled the Earth around fifty million years ago, but the domestic cat that we know today is directly descended from the African cat, which first appeared about 130,000 years ago and still survives today.

2. Cats began to be kept by humans at least 10,000 years ago, probably to protect stores of precious food from mice and rats.

3. The ancient Egyptians worshipped their cats, and when the animals died many were put in the temple of Bastet, the goddess of cats.

Bastet, the Egyptian goddess of cats

4. Killing cats was a crime in ancient Egypt, for which the punishment was death.

5. Sea-faring traders took cats from Africa across the Mediterranean Sea to Italy about 3,000 years ago, from where the animals spread across the rest of Europe.

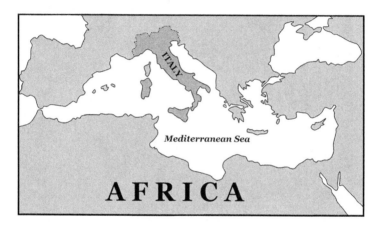

6. Cats arrived in Britain around 1,000 years ago and were taken to America when the Atlantic Ocean was crossed 700 years later.

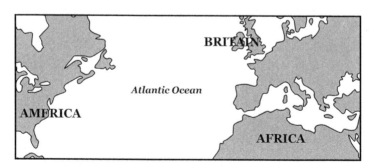

7.   During the Middle Ages in Europe, cats - black ones in particular - became associated with the devil and witches. Many cats were killed to ward off evil, and were thrown on bonfires during the period of Lent.

8.   The Black Death swept through Europe in the fourteenth century killing millions of people. It was spread by black rats, and it is thought that the reason the Black Death was so devastating was because there were so few cats to catch the rats.

9. It wasn't until the seventeenth century that cats became accepted again by humans, and today the cat is the most popular type of pet in the world.

Body Types

10. Cats come in a number of different basic body types, with "Foreign" and "Cobby" being at the two different extremes of shape.

11. The "Foreign" body shape evolved in warmer parts of the world, as its slim body helps to get rid of heat. It has a long thin tail, long legs, a wedge-shaped head, and large ears.

The "Foreign" cat shape

12. The "Cobby" body shape evolved in colder parts of the world, as its thickset body helps to retain heat. It has a thick round tail, short legs, a broad head, and small ears.

The "Cobby" cat shape

13. Most cats are neither completely cobby nor foreign shaped, but have a body shape somewhere between the two.

Anatomy

The Skeleton

14. Cats have around 244 bones in their bodies. This number will vary depending on the length of a cat's tail or if it has extra toes.

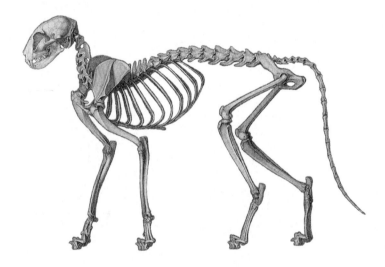

The cat skeleton

15. Cats have very flexible spines. This is because they have around twenty more bones - or "vertebrae" - in them than human ones. These vertebrae are joined together by muscle, which is much more flexible than the ligaments that connect the bones in a human spine.

16. In the human skeleton the shoulder blades are connected to the spine by the collarbones. In a cat's skeleton though, these bones aren't connected, but are supported by muscles. This helps with flexibility and means that the cat can squeeze through spaces that seem too small.

17. The bones in a cat's skeleton are both light and strong. The lightness allows a cat to move and change direction at high speed, and the strength means it can land heavily without getting hurt.

Muscles

18. A cat's muscles are both strong and flexible, enabling it to curl up tightly into a ball and to jump many times its own height.

19. Cats can turn their ears through 180° to face forward or backward, thanks to the thirty-two muscles they have in each ear. A human ear has just six muscles.

20. Cats are excellent hunters and their muscles have evolved so that they can stalk their prey silently before pouncing on it in a burst of energy. The powerful muscles in the jaw then enable the cat to easily slice through its victim.

A stalking cat

21. A cat's muscles tire out easily, so although a cat can run at speeds of up to thirty miles per hour (50 kph) and jump like an acrobat, it can't do these activities for long periods.

<u>Fur</u>

22. The fur which covers a cat's skin provides protection against cold, heat, and water.

23. The patterns and colors of a cat's fur allows it to blend into its surroundings when hunting.

24. There are three types of hair in a cat's coat. "Guard hairs," which form a tough outer layer and repel water, "Awn hairs," which help with protection, and "Down hairs," which trap air to keep in warmth.

25. A special type of hair on a cat is the whiskers. They connect to nerves deep below the skin and are very sensitive. They allow a cat to find its way around in the dark.

26. Whiskers aren't just found on a cat's face, but also on the back of its legs.

Paws & Claws

27. A cat's paws and claws cushion the impact when jumping or running, and are also used for fighting, climbing trees, and catching prey.

28. On each paw are soft pads which allow the cat to walk as silently as possible.

The pads on a cat's paw

29. A cat's paws are designed so that it walks on its toes, which means it is ready to jump into action the moment it needs to.

30. Cats have four toes on each back paw and five toes on each front paw.

31. Each toe has a claw tucked inside which can be extended out when needed. This helps the cat to walk silently, and also helps to keep its claws sharp.

Eyes

32. A cat's eye works in the same way as a human's, but has evolved to see better in the dark, as cats do most of their hunting during twilight, and at dawn and dusk.

33. As in the human eye, the pupil changes size to allow more or less light in. The pupil of a cat's eye, though, also changes shape from a narrow slit to a large circle. This allows the cat to see clearly in both bright sunshine and near darkness.

34. Cats have a layer of special cells at the back of the eye which acts like a mirror, reflecting light back into the eye. This is why a cat's eye seems to gleam in the dark.

Teeth

35. A cat has thirty teeth of which there are three types, each one designed for a different purpose.

A cat shows its teeth

36. There are four long, dagger-like canine teeth which hold and kill the cat's prey.

37. The twelve small incisors at the front of the mouth are designed to rip the flesh from the bones of the cat's victim.

38. The fourteen molars at the back of the mouth are used to slice the flesh into pieces small enough for the cat to swallow.

Senses

Hearing

39. Cats have remarkable hearing. They can hear much higher sounds than humans and even dogs, which is very useful when hunting small rodents!

40. Because a cat can move its ears through 180°, each one separately, it can hear sounds from all directions without moving its head.

41. Cats can tell the difference between very similar sounds. They can tell which family member is walking towards them by the sound of their footsteps, or they can tell which cupboard you are opening in the kitchen by the sound of the door. They can even tell if it's your car approaching by the sound of the engine!

Sight

42. Because cats hunt mostly at dawn or dusk, their sight has evolved to see much better in the dark than humans, although they can't see color and details as well as us. But the most important thing for a cat when hunting is to be able to spot the movement of its prey - when it's dark, color and detail aren't important.

43. Although a cat has a wider field of vision than a human, its eyes can't see behind its head.

To see in this blind spot, it can move its head nearly all the way round, much like an owl.

Smell

44.   The sense of smell is very important to a cat. Unlike a dog, which uses its nose when hunting, a cat uses its sense of smell for communicating, to find food, and to tell if food is safe to eat.

45.   As well as using its nose to smell, a cat has an organ in its mouth, called the "vomeronasal organ," which can collect information about a scent.

46.   A cat's sense of smell is about fourteen times stronger than a human's. If a teaspoon of salt, which humans find odorless, is dissolved in one gallon (4.5 litres) of water, a cat will be able to smell the difference between that and a gallon of plain water.

Behavior & Instinct

<u>Sleep</u>

47.   Being hunters by nature, cats need to conserve their energy, and for this reason they spend around sixteen hours asleep every day. This is not continuous sleeping, but a series of short "catnaps."

48.   Even when deeply asleep, a cat's brain remains alert to any signs of danger.

49.   There is evidence that cats have dreams when they are asleep. A cat is probably dreaming if its whiskers and ears are twitching or its paws and claws are moving.

Hunting

50.   Although cats are natural hunters, they are not completely instinctive - a kitten needs to be taught by its mother or another cat.

51.   When a cat is hunting, it is alerted to a suitable victim by movement. It then approaches slowly, keeping low to the ground with fixed eyes and alert ears.

52.   If a cat has to cross open space while stalking its prey, it travels forward quickly with its body pressed close to the ground. This is known as the "slink run." The cat pauses every now and then to stare at its prey before continuing.

53.   When the cat is close to its victim, it crouches down, treading with its back legs before pouncing on its prey.

54.   Pet cats have no need to hunt for food as they are fed regularly by their owners, but the instinct is deep-rooted. When they are playing with a toy or another cat, they are practising their hunting skills.

Territory

55.   All cats have an instinct to mark and defend their territory. The size of their territory depends on how many cats there are in the area and how much space is available.

56. Cats leave a scent to mark their territory by spraying urine. Other cats can tell by the scent of the urine that this territory belongs to another cat.

57. Another way a cat can leave its scent is by rubbing its head and body against objects. The scent comes from glands in the skin. Glands on the pads of the paws also leave a scent when a cat scratches a tree or a wooden post.

Grooming

58. Cats spend a lot of time grooming themselves by licking their coats. This gets rid of loose hair and smooths the fur to provide better insulation. The tongue is covered in spines which makes it a very good comb.

59. Grooming also stimulates glands that makes the coat waterproof. In hot weather, the saliva that the cat puts on its coat evaporates, keeping the cat cool.

Birth & Kittens

60. A female cat will be pregnant for about nine weeks before giving birth to her litter of kittens. Producing between four and six kittens is normal for a cat, although litters of up to eight are not unusual.

A mother and her kitten

61. When a kitten is born, its eyes are closed and its ears are folded back, so it is unable to see or hear and is totally dependent on its mother. It feeds on its mother's milk for the first four weeks of its life.

62. Cats make excellent mothers. They spend all their time with their kittens for the first few days; feeding, grooming, and protecting them.

Later on they teach their offspring all the skills they need to survive as an adult cat.

63. By the second week of its life, a kitten may be taking its first steps, although it will be unsteady on its feet. Its eyes will start to open and its ears will begin to unfold.

64. By the third week, a kitten is walking confidently, starting to explore, and playing with its brothers and sisters. The mother gets them used to being on their own by leaving them for brief periods.

Kittens playing

65. A kitten grows very quickly, and when it is three months old it will be fully independent. In the wild though, a female kitten may stay with her mother until she produces kittens of her own. A male kitten will leave the family to find territory of his own.

Cat Types

66. There are over 100 different breeds of cats, which have been developed over the years to come in many colors, shapes, and sizes. Unlike dogs, which are bred to perform different tasks, cats are bred purely for how they look.

67. Most cats are not a pure breed, they will be simply short-haired moggies, or crossbreeds, which have inherited the best qualities from many different types of cat.

68. Cats have different types of coat. They can be long-haired, semi-long-haired, or short-haired; and these coats come in a variety of colors and patterns.

69. All kittens are born with blue eyes, but by the time they reach adulthood they will have changed color to anything from a wide range of different shades of blue, brown, yellow, or green.

70. A cat's eyes can be one of three shapes, round, almond, or slanted.

Almond Eyes

Round Eyes

Slanting Eyes

Assorted Cat Facts

71. There are more than 500 million cats kept as pets world-wide.

72. In October, 1963, a cat called Félicette became the first cat in space aboard a French rocket, surviving a fifteen-minute flight. Felix should have been the first cat to go into space, but he escaped before the launch.

73. The largest litter ever produced by a cat was nineteen kittens, although four of them died.

74. Many people think that cats can see in the dark, but in total darkness they are as blind as we are. What they can do is see well when there is just the faintest amount of light.

75. It is not unusual for a cat to live to around twenty years old. This is the equivalent of about ninety-six human years.

76. The oldest known cat was called Crème Puff which lived in Austin, Texas. She died in August, 2005, aged thirty-eight years and three days.

77. The tail is used to help with balance and contains one tenth of a cat's bones.

78. Cats are great at climbing trees, but their claws curve the wrong way for coming down gracefully. They have to slither down backwards relying on their claws to hold their weight.

79. Cats are highly sensitive to vibration and it seems that they can predict earthquakes and volcano eruptions. They can detect the first, faint tremors, which can't be felt by humans.

80. Cats saved many lives in Britain during World War Two because of their superior hearing. They could hear enemy aircraft coming before humans, and when they ran for cover their owners followed them to safety.

Illustration Attributions

Bastet, the Egyptian goddess of cats
Gunawan Kartapranata [CC BY-SA 3.0
(https://creativecommons.org/licenses/by-sa/3.0)]B

Black rat (Fact 8)
www.publicdomainpictures.net
CC0 Public Domain

The cat skeleton
Hercule Straus-Durkheim [Public domain]

Printed in Great Britain
by Amazon

15451890R00020